SOUTH AMERIC.. ᴄʀᴜɪꜱᴇ
GUIDE 2025.

![cruise port photograph]

A Journey Through South America's Spectacular Coasts, Cities, and Wildlife

ALBERT R. WEIMER

COPYRIGHT

PREFACE

Welcome to the South America Cruise Guide 2025, your essential companion to exploring one of the most diverse and captivating regions on Earth. Whether you're a first-time cruiser or a seasoned traveler, this guide will help you navigate the stunning landscapes, vibrant cities, and rich cultures that make South America a must-visit destination for any cruise enthusiast.

South America is a continent brimming with extraordinary contrasts. From the lush rainforests of the Amazon to the towering peaks of the Andes, from the cosmopolitan charm of Buenos Aires to the serene beauty of the Galápagos Islands, the region offers a wealth of experiences for every traveler. Whether you're drawn to ancient ruins, thriving metropolises, or untouched natural wonders, South America has something to satisfy your wanderlust.

This guide has been carefully curated to provide you with all the essential information you need to make the most of your South America cruise. From detailed itineraries and recommendations on the best cruise lines to shore excursions, dining, and cultural highlights, you'll find everything you need to plan an unforgettable journey.

The pages ahead will take you on a journey through iconic destinations such as Rio de Janeiro, the Antarctic Peninsula, and the fascinating coastline of Chile. Alongside these famous stops, we'll also introduce you to hidden gems that lie off the beaten path, offering you a unique and enriching perspective of this incredible continent.

As you embark on your South American adventure, I hope this guide helps you discover not only the beauty of the landscape but also the warmth and hospitality of its people. South America's cultural richness, history, and natural wonders await, and this guide will ensure you make the most of your time in this dynamic part of the world

TABLE OF CONTENTS

CHAPTER 1: INTRODUCTION

Why Choose a South America Cruise?

A South America cruise is one of the most thrilling and rewarding ways to explore this dynamic and diverse continent. Whether you're an avid adventurer, a culture enthusiast, or someone who loves scenic beauty, South America offers an eclectic mix of landscapes, wildlife, and cultures that are bound to capture your imagination. With a cruise, you can experience multiple countries, unique destinations, and a variety of shore excursions, all while enjoying the luxury and convenience of a floating hotel.

South America is a continent that is as vast as it is diverse. From the tropical jungles of the Amazon to the icy wonders of

Patagonia, from the colorful streets of Rio de Janeiro to the historic ruins of Machu Picchu, a South America cruise covers a wide spectrum of experiences. Whether you're seeking adventure, relaxation, or cultural exploration, a cruise through South America offers something for every type of traveler.

Overview of the Region

South America, the fourth largest continent in the world, is bordered by the Pacific Ocean to the west, the Atlantic Ocean to the east, and the Caribbean Sea to the north. With countries like Argentina, Brazil, Chile, Peru, Ecuador, and Uruguay, each region offers its own distinct charm and beauty.

The Amazon Basin: This vast, biodiverse region, mostly located in Brazil, is home to the world's largest rainforest and river system. It's a place of mystery and adventure, with dense jungle, exotic wildlife, and indigenous tribes that have lived here for centuries.

Patagonia: Spanning the southern parts of Argentina and Chile, Patagonia is a land of glaciers, rugged mountains, and wildlife. It's the perfect destination for those seeking outdoor adventures like hiking, kayaking, and exploring vast, untouched landscapes.

The Andes Mountains: Running along the western edge of South America, the Andes offer breathtaking views and challenging hikes, including visits to high-altitude cities like **Quito** and **La Paz**, as well as famous archaeological sites like **Machu Picchu** in Peru.

Brazil: Brazil is a vibrant country, known for its lively cities, like **Rio de Janeiro** and **Sao Paulo**, and iconic landmarks like **Christ the Redeemer**. It's also famous for its stunning coastline, which offers sandy beaches, the lush Amazon rainforest, and a rich culture steeped in music and dance.

The Galápagos Islands: Located off the coast of Ecuador, the Galápagos offer a wildlife lover's dream come true. This archipelago is home to unique species found nowhere else in the world, and cruising through these islands is an incredible way to see creatures like giant tortoises, marine iguanas, and blue-footed boobies up close.

Each region has its own character and is waiting to be explored by sea. A South American cruise allows you to seamlessly transition from one diverse destination to the next, all while enjoying world-class amenities aboard your ship.

Unique Experiences on a South America Cruise

One of the major draws of a South America cruise is the unique, once-in-a-lifetime experiences that you can't easily replicate elsewhere. A cruise allows you to explore various environments in a way that would be difficult to accomplish by land travel alone. Here are some of the standout experiences you can expect:

Wildlife Encounters:

In the **Galápagos Islands**, you can swim with sea lions, watch giant tortoises roam freely, or observe marine iguanas basking in the sun.

In the **Amazon Rainforest**, you might spot pink river dolphins, sloths, monkeys, and countless species of birds in their natural habitats, often from small boats as you glide along the river's tributaries.

Patagonia offers amazing opportunities for wildlife watching, including penguin colonies, guanacos (relatives of llamas), and the elusive puma in remote areas.

Cultural Immersion:

South America's cities are a melting pot of culture. You can visit historic landmarks like **Machu Picchu** and **Easter Island** in Chile or enjoy vibrant festivals like **Carnival** in Brazil, where samba parades and street parties take over the streets.

Learn the art of **tango dancing** in Buenos Aires or sample Argentina's world-renowned wine while touring its vineyards in Mendoza.

Adventure and Outdoor Activities:

Whether you're hiking on a glacier in **Patagonia**, cruising through the fjords of **Chile**, or zip-lining through the jungle canopy in **Costa Rica**, South America offers a vast playground for adventure enthusiasts.

You can go kayaking or snorkeling in the clear waters of the **Galápagos Islands**, trek through ancient Inca trails, or explore the towering peaks of the **Andes Mountains**.

Stunning Scenic Landscapes:

A cruise through the **Chilean Fjords** offers spectacular views of snow-capped peaks, glaciers, and pristine waters. As you sail through these remote regions, you'll be treated to some of the most awe-inspiring scenery on the planet.

A journey through **Patagonia** provides incredible vistas of icebergs, glaciers, and expansive plains, perfect for nature lovers and photographers.

World-Class Cuisine and Wine:

South America is a haven for foodies, offering delicious and diverse culinary experiences. Savor **Argentinian steaks**,

Brazilian feijoada (a savory bean stew), or fresh seafood from the Pacific coast of Chile.

The region is also known for its excellent wine, particularly in countries like **Argentina** and **Chile**, where you can take wine-tasting tours in the scenic vineyards of Mendoza or the Maipo Valley.

Luxury and Comfort:

South American cruises combine the thrill of exploration with the luxury of cruising. Cruise ships offer a range of accommodations from comfortable staterooms to lavish suites, as well as fine dining, entertainment, and spas. After a day of adventure, you can relax onboard with world-class amenities while enjoying stunning views of South America's diverse landscapes.

Best Time to Visit

The best time to cruise South America depends largely on the regions you plan to visit. South America's climate varies widely due to its size and geography, which means that there's no one-size-fits-all answer for the ideal travel period. However, here's a general guide to help you choose the best time to visit based on your interests and the regions you're exploring:

The Amazon Rainforest (Brazil):

Best Time: The dry season, from **June to November**, is ideal for cruising the Amazon. The water levels are lower during this time, which allows for more accessible exploration of tributaries and waterways. The weather is warmer and less humid, with fewer mosquitoes than during the rainy season.

Patagonia (Argentina and Chile):

Best Time: The best time to visit Patagonia is during the Southern Hemisphere's summer months, from **December to March**. These months offer warmer weather and longer days, perfect for outdoor activities and exploration. However, even in summer, the weather in Patagonia can be unpredictable, so it's essential to be prepared for changes in temperature.

Galápagos Islands (Ecuador):

Best Time: The Galápagos can be visited year-round, but the **cooler season from June to November** is often considered the best time for wildlife viewing. During these months, the waters are cooler, which brings more nutrients and attracts an abundance of marine life, making it a fantastic time for snorkeling and diving.

Brazil (Rio de Janeiro, Salvador, and the Amazon):

Best Time: December to March is the best time to visit Brazil for beach lovers and those looking to enjoy the famous **Carnival** season (usually in February or March). However, the peak summer months can be hot and humid, particularly in the Amazon. The cooler and less crowded months of **April to October** are perfect for those who want to explore the cities and national parks without the intense heat.

Chilean Fjords:

Best Time: The best time to visit the Chilean Fjords is during the **Southern Hemisphere summer (November to March)**. During this time, the weather is milder, and the daylight hours are longer, allowing for better visibility of the spectacular scenery.

Andes Mountains (Peru, Bolivia, Ecuador):

Best Time: **May to September** is the dry season in the Andean regions, and it's the best time to visit for trekking, hiking, and exploring high-altitude sites like **Machu Picchu**. The weather is cooler, but the skies are usually clear, and the trails are more accessible.

CHAPTER 2: TOP SOUTH AMERICAN CRUISE DESTINATIONS

A South American cruise is a gateway to some of the most stunning and diverse destinations in the world. From tropical rainforests to icy fjords, and from bustling cities to isolated archipelagos, the region offers something for every type of traveler. This chapter explores some of the most popular and iconic cruise destinations in South America, each offering its own unique experiences and attractions.

The Amazon River: A Journey Through the Heart of the Jungle

The Amazon River, often referred to as the "lungs of the Earth," is one of the most unique and captivating destinations you can explore on a South American cruise. Spanning across nine countries, with the majority of it located in Brazil, this vast river system is the lifeblood of the Amazon Rainforest, home to one of the most biodiverse ecosystems on the planet.

Cruising the Amazon is a once-in-a-lifetime experience. Travelers can navigate the river's winding tributaries, experiencing the jungle from the comfort of a luxurious river cruise ship. As you cruise through the dense rainforest, you'll encounter wildlife such as pink river dolphins, caimans, toucans, and monkeys. The region is also home to numerous indigenous tribes, some of whom still live in remote villages along the river. Visiting these communities offers a fascinating insight into their way of life, traditions, and relationship with the land.

Besides wildlife and indigenous cultures, the Amazon offers natural wonders that are unlike anything else on Earth. A sunrise or sunset over the river, with the sounds of the jungle in the background, is an unforgettable experience. Excursions often include activities like jungle treks, canoe trips to spot wildlife, and visits to remote villages, offering travelers a deep connection with one of the world's most pristine environments.

Buenos Aires, Argentina: Vibrancy and Culture

Buenos Aires, the capital of Argentina, is one of South America's most exciting cities, brimming with cultural attractions, lively streets, and world-class dining. A visit to

Buenos Aires is a cultural immersion, where you can experience the passionate tango, explore colonial architecture, and indulge in some of the best steaks on the planet.

The city is often called the "Paris of South America" because of its European-style boulevards, stunning architecture, and cultural flair. The city's neighborhoods, each with its own distinct personality, offer plenty to explore. In San Telmo, cobbled streets are lined with antique shops and tango dancers, while Palermo is known for its trendy cafes, boutiques, and green spaces. For a glimpse of the city's historical and political heart, visit the iconic Plaza de

Mayo and the Casa Rosada, Argentina's presidential palace.

Buenos Aires is also a food lover's paradise. The Argentine steak is world-famous, and no trip is complete without dining at one of the city's many parrillas (steakhouses). Don't forget to try other local specialties such as empanadas, choripán, and dulce de leche desserts. The city's vibrant culinary scene is an essential part of the Buenos Aires experience, making it an ideal stop on any South American cruise.

Chilean Fjords: Majestic Landscapes and Natural Wonders

The Chilean Fjords are one of South America's most spectacular natural wonders, offering some of the most dramatic and untouched landscapes on Earth. Located along the southern coast of Chile, this network of fjords, glaciers, and islands is an adventure lover's dream, with a wide range of outdoor activities and breathtaking scenery.

Cruising through the Chilean Fjords is an awe-inspiring experience, where towering mountains rise from the sea and glaciers tumble down into the water. One of the most iconic stops is the famous Torres del Paine National Park, a UNESCO World Heritage site known for its jagged peaks, turquoise lakes, and abundant wildlife, including guanacos and condors. The area is also a haven for those who enjoy hiking, photography, and nature walks.

As your ship navigates the fjords, you'll pass through serene waters surrounded by snow-capped mountains, with waterfalls cascading down the cliffs. You may also have the chance to see glaciers calving into the ocean, an incredible sight that will leave you in awe of nature's power. The Chilean Fjords are remote and pristine, offering an unparalleled chance to connect with nature in one of the world's last untouched wilderness areas.

Rio de Janeiro, Brazil: Beaches, Carnival, and Iconic Sights

Rio de Janeiro is one of South America's most famous and exciting cities, offering a perfect blend of stunning natural beauty, rich culture, and vibrant nightlife. Situated on Brazil's southeastern coast, Rio is known for its beautiful beaches, dramatic mountain scenery, and world-famous landmarks like the Christ the Redeemer statue.

The city is synonymous with fun, and there's no better place to experience Brazil's lively culture than Rio. The famous Copacabana and Ipanema beaches are perfect spots to relax, soak up the sun, or enjoy water sports like surfing and beach volleyball. For those looking for adventure, a hike to the top of Sugarloaf Mountain offers panoramic views of the city and coastline. The view of Rio's bays and mountains is truly breathtaking, with the city sprawled beneath you.

Rio is also renowned for its Carnival, one of the largest and most spectacular festivals in the world. If you're cruising during Carnival season (usually in February or March), you may have the chance to witness the colorful parades, samba performances, and street parties that make Rio de Janeiro the epicenter of celebration in Brazil.

Of course, Rio is also home to significant cultural landmarks. Christ the Redeemer, one of the New Seven Wonders of the World, is a must-see. The iconic statue stands atop Corcovado Mountain, offering incredible views of the city and surrounding bay.

Galápagos Islands, Ecuador: Wildlife Adventure

For nature lovers and wildlife enthusiasts, a visit to the Galápagos Islands is an extraordinary opportunity to encounter some of the most unique and diverse species on Earth. Located off the coast of Ecuador, the Galápagos archipelago consists of 13 major islands, each with its own ecosystem and wildlife.

Cruising to the Galápagos is like stepping back in time to a natural world untouched by human development. The islands are home to a variety of endemic species, including giant tortoises, marine iguanas, and the famous Darwin's finches. The Galápagos offer an exceptional opportunity for wildlife observation, and visitors can get up close and personal with animals that are found nowhere else in the world.

The Galápagos Islands are also a haven for outdoor activities. Visitors can snorkel with sea lions, kayak along pristine shores, and hike volcanic landscapes. The archipelago is a UNESCO World Heritage site and offers an incredibly well-preserved environment, making it one of the most exceptional cruise destinations in the world.

Patagonia: Rugged Beauty and Exploration

Patagonia, a vast region spanning the southernmost parts of Chile and Argentina, is one of the world's last frontiers. With its jagged peaks, glaciers, and remote wilderness, Patagonia is an adventurer's paradise, offering some of the most striking natural landscapes in South America.

Cruising through Patagonia is a journey into a land of raw, untamed beauty. The region is famous for its dramatic mountain ranges, such as the Andes and the Southern Ice Field, and is home to awe-inspiring national parks like Los Glaciares in

Argentina and Torres del Paine in Chile. Glaciers such as Perito Moreno, one of the world's few advancing glaciers, provide an unforgettable spectacle as they calve large chunks of ice into the waters below.

Patagonia also offers numerous opportunities for outdoor activities like trekking, kayaking, and wildlife watching. The region's rugged beauty and isolation make it an ideal destination for travelers seeking adventure in the wild.

CHAPTER 3: TOP SOUTH AMERICAN CRUISE DESTINATIONS

South America is a continent of contrasts and extremes, making it a dream destination for cruise travelers. From the lush, untamed wilds of the Amazon Rainforest to the rugged, glacial beauty of Patagonia, there is no shortage of spectacular destinations to explore. In this chapter, we'll explore the top cruise destinations across the continent, highlighting the best experiences, activities, and reasons why these places should be on your South American cruise itinerary.

The Amazon River: A Journey Through the Heart of the Jungle

The Amazon River is perhaps the most iconic of all South American destinations. Spanning over 4,000 miles and draining into the Atlantic Ocean, the Amazon is the world's largest river by volume, flowing through several countries, including Brazil, Peru, Colombia, Ecuador, and Venezuela. However, the Brazilian stretch of the Amazon remains the most visited by cruise ships.

A Living Ecosystem

The Amazon isn't just a river—it's an ecosystem. It's one of the most biodiverse places on Earth, home to over 10% of the world's known species. Cruising through the Amazon offers a front-row seat to this vibrant natural world. As your ship glides through the murky waters of the river, you'll have the opportunity to spot pink dolphins, caimans, sloths, monkeys, and countless bird species. Whether it's the rare harpy eagle or the colorful macaw, the Amazon is a paradise for birdwatchers and wildlife enthusiasts.

Life Along the River

The Amazon River is also a lifeline for the communities that live along its banks. Many cruise itineraries include stops in these remote villages, where visitors can interact with indigenous tribes, learn about their customs, and gain a deeper understanding of the region's cultural history. This interaction provides a unique and enriching experience, as travelers get to learn firsthand how these communities have adapted to life in the jungle over centuries.

Excursions and Activities

There are numerous excursions available to those exploring the Amazon by cruise. One of the most popular activities is to take small boats or canoes into the heart of the rainforest for a closer look at the flora and fauna. These excursions might involve fishing for piranhas, hiking through dense jungle trails, or visiting local markets to buy handmade crafts. For those seeking an adrenaline rush, some itineraries offer night safaris, where the jungle comes alive with nocturnal creatures.

The Amazon is one of the world's most remote and untouched regions, offering a level of isolation and natural beauty few places can match. Whether you're interested in nature, culture, or simply the thrill of exploring a world-famous wilderness, the Amazon River is a must-see destination on any South American cruise.

Buenos Aires, Argentina: Vibrancy and Culture

Buenos Aires is the heartbeat of Argentina, a cosmopolitan city with a blend of European elegance and Latin American flair. Known for its tango music, lively neighborhoods, and rich cultural scene, Buenos Aires offers a dynamic stop on any South American cruise. Whether you're exploring the iconic landmarks, sampling local delicacies, or enjoying a tango show, there's always something happening in this energetic city.

A Cultural Hotspot

Buenos Aires is often referred to as the "Paris of South America" due to its wide boulevards, French-inspired architecture, and sophisticated cultural offerings. A visit to this Argentine capital is a sensory experience. You'll find a wealth of museums, theaters, galleries, and performance venues. The Teatro Colón, one of the world's most famous opera houses, offers guided tours and performances that are not to be missed. For history buffs, the

Museum of Latin American Art of Buenos Aires (MALBA) features impressive collections of contemporary Latin American art.

The city's rich history can be explored in neighborhoods like San Telmo, a charming area filled with cobblestone streets, colonial buildings, and antique shops. It's the best place to experience the cultural heartbeat of Buenos Aires, from tango performances to lively cafés. For a more modern vibe, head to Palermo, an area known for its trendy cafes, boutiques, and large green spaces.

Food and Drink

Argentine cuisine is world-renowned, and Buenos Aires is the perfect place to indulge. The city's parrillas (steakhouses) serve up some of the best steaks in the world, including the famous Argentine beef. A visit to Buenos Aires wouldn't be complete without enjoying a classic Argentine barbecue, or "asado," where various cuts of meat are grilled to perfection.

Besides steaks, you can also sample traditional Argentine dishes like empanadas (stuffed pastries), choripán (a type of sausage sandwich), and milanesa (breaded meat cutlets). Don't forget to try the city's famous dulce de leche desserts, such as alfajores (cookies filled with caramel) or chocotorta (a chocolate and dulce de leche cake).

Tango: The Dance of Buenos Aires

Buenos Aires is the birthplace of tango, and no visit to the city is complete without experiencing this passionate and evocative dance. Travelers can watch tango performances in iconic venues like Café Tortoni or the more traditional tango houses, where local dancers perform intimate shows. For those who want to try the dance themselves, there are plenty of tango schools throughout the city offering lessons for beginners and seasoned dancers alike.

Chilean Fjords: Majestic Landscapes and Natural Wonders

The Chilean Fjords are one of South America's most awe-inspiring natural destinations. Located along the southern coast of Chile, the fjords offer an unparalleled view of untouched wilderness, with glaciers, waterfalls, and towering mountains.

A Remote and Pristine Wilderness

Cruising through the Chilean Fjords is like stepping into a postcard. As your ship winds through the fjords, you'll be surrounded by jagged cliffs, verdant forests, and snowy peaks. The region is remote, and its isolation has helped preserve its raw beauty. The fjords are dotted with small islands, each with its own unique ecosystem and wildlife. Some ships venture into areas that are only accessible by boat, allowing passengers to experience the pristine beauty of this unspoiled region.

The Chilean Fjords are also home to several famous national parks, such as Torres del Paine National Park, which offers some of the best hiking and trekking opportunities in South America. The park is known for its towering granite spires, turquoise lakes, and diverse wildlife, including guanacos (wild relatives of llamas), foxes, and condors.

Glaciers and Waterfalls

One of the highlights of a Chilean Fjords cruise is the opportunity to witness massive glaciers in person. The Pio XI Glacier, the largest glacier in the Southern Hemisphere, is a breathtaking sight. Visitors can also see smaller glaciers calving into the sea, sending huge chunks of ice crashing into the water below. The fjords are also home to stunning waterfalls that cascade down the cliffs, creating a mesmerizing and tranquil atmosphere.

For those looking to explore on foot, the fjords offer a number of hiking trails that lead to panoramic viewpoints where you can gaze out over the pristine wilderness below.

Rio de Janeiro, Brazil: Beaches, Carnival, and Iconic Sights

Rio de Janeiro is perhaps one of the most well-known cities in South America, famed for its vibrant culture, stunning beaches, and iconic landmarks. Known as the "Cidade Maravilhosa" (Marvelous City), Rio offers a perfect combination of natural beauty, world-class attractions, and lively festivities.

Iconic Landmarks

No visit to Rio de Janeiro would be complete without seeing the Christ the Redeemer statue, one of the New Seven

Wonders of the World. Perched atop Corcovado Mountain, the statue offers breathtaking views of the city, including the famous Sugarloaf Mountain and the sprawling beaches below. You can either hike up to the statue or take a train that winds its way through the lush Tijuca Forest.

Another must-see landmark is the Sugarloaf Mountain, a granite peak that rises above the bay. Visitors can take a cable car to the summit, where they'll be treated to sweeping views of the city, beaches, and surrounding mountains.

Beaches and Outdoor Activities

Rio de Janeiro is home to some of the world's most famous beaches, including Copacabana and Ipanema. These golden stretches of sand are perfect for relaxing, people-watching, and enjoying the beautiful weather. Visitors can join in beach sports such as volleyball and footvolley or simply lounge under an umbrella with a cold coconut drink.

For the more adventurous traveler, Rio offers plenty of outdoor activities. Hiking to the top of the Dois Irmãos (Two Brothers) peaks provides spectacular views of the city, while visitors can also try their hand at surfing at one of the city's many surf breaks.

Carnival

Perhaps the most famous of all Rio's attractions is the Carnival, a vibrant festival that takes place every year before Lent. During this period, the streets come alive with music, dancing, and colorful parades. The samba schools of Rio perform in the Sambadrome, showcasing elaborate floats, costumes, and performances that are a feast for the eyes.

If your cruise coincides with Carnival, you'll experience one of the world's largest and most spectacular festivals, a true celebration of Brazilian culture and spirit.

CHAPTER 4: CRUISE LINES AND SHIPS OPERATING IN SOUTH AMERICA

When planning a cruise to South America, choosing the right cruise line and ship can significantly enhance your travel experience. Different cruise lines offer varying itineraries, services, and levels of luxury, so understanding the options available to you is crucial to ensuring that your cruise is tailored to your needs. In this chapter, we will explore the most prominent cruise lines operating in South America, the types of ships they use, and what you can expect in terms of onboard experiences

Popular Cruise Lines Operating in South America

Several major cruise lines offer journeys through South America, each bringing something unique to the table. Whether you're looking for a luxurious all-inclusive experience or a more adventurous voyage to explore remote wilderness, the right cruise line can provide it. Below, we'll break down some of the most popular cruise lines operating in the region.

Celebrity Cruises

Celebrity Cruises is known for its premium service and elegant ships. The line operates a variety of itineraries that explore South America's coasts, including trips to Argentina, Chile, Brazil, and the Galápagos Islands. With Celebrity Cruises, travelers can enjoy a blend of relaxation, luxury, and exciting shore excursions.

Itineraries: Celebrity Cruises offers both shorter, more relaxed itineraries and longer, more adventurous cruises that focus on remote locations like the Galápagos. Popular routes include cruises to Buenos Aires, Rio de Janeiro, Valparaiso, and the Falkland Islands.

Ship Features: Celebrity ships are known for their modern, stylish décor and world-class amenities. The cruise line's fleet includes large, luxurious ships like the **Celebrity Eclipse**, which are equipped with a variety of onboard entertainment options, specialty dining venues, and wellness facilities like spas and fitness centers.

Experience: Celebrity Cruises is perfect for those who want to enjoy a balance of luxury with immersive destination experiences. The line offers both cultural and wildlife-focused excursions, with a particular emphasis on offering high-end service and accommodations. Celebrity also has a reputation for catering to foodies, offering gourmet dining with wine pairings that emphasize regional specialties.

Princess Cruises

Princess Cruises is one of the largest and most popular cruise lines worldwide, and it has a significant presence in South America. Known for its classic cruising experience, Princess Cruises offers a range of itineraries for those looking to explore South America at a leisurely pace.

Itineraries: Princess Cruises offers both South American coastal cruises and longer, more extensive voyages that might even include the Panama Canal. Common stops include Buenos Aires, Rio de Janeiro, Montevideo, and the Chilean Fjords. Princess Cruises also features voyages that combine South America with Antarctica for travelers looking for a more epic adventure.

Ship Features: Princess ships like the **Diamond Princess** and **Crown Princess** offer spacious staterooms, multiple pools, expansive open decks for viewing, and a wide variety of dining options. Princess is particularly known for its "Movies Under the Stars" outdoor theater, where passengers can enjoy films on a big screen while relaxing by the pool.

Experience: Known for its mid-range luxury, Princess Cruises offers an experience suitable for families, couples, and solo travelers alike. The onboard activities are broad, from relaxation-focused amenities like spas and hot tubs to more active options like fitness classes, dance lessons, and casino gaming. Princess Cruises also provides excellent shore excursions, including wildlife safaris in Patagonia and trips to the Falkland Islands.

Holland America Line

Holland America Line is known for offering premium cruise experiences, with a strong focus on culture and exploration. The line offers longer itineraries that delve deeply into the heart of South America, offering more immersive experiences for travelers.

Itineraries: Holland America operates cruises that explore the coasts of Argentina, Chile, and Brazil, as well as offering longer routes that venture down to Antarctica. Their cruises are ideal for those seeking a more culturally immersive experience or those looking to explore the less-visited areas of South America, such as the Galápagos and the Amazon River.

Ship Features: Holland America ships like the **MS Zaandam** and **MS Rotterdam** are elegant yet comfortable. They feature a classic cruise experience with luxurious décor, fine dining, and top-notch service. The ships also feature spacious public areas, lounges, theaters, and a robust enrichment program, which includes lectures and cultural performances related to the ports of call.

Experience: Holland America is well-suited for more mature travelers or those looking for a refined cruise experience. The ship's amenities include high-end dining, an extensive selection of shore excursions, and an emphasis on enrichment activities. The cruise line also offers exclusive excursions to remote parts of South America, such as Patagonia and the Amazon.

MSC Cruises

MSC Cruises is a European-based cruise line that has become increasingly popular in South America. Known for offering a blend of European style with South American flair, MSC offers both family-friendly and luxury cruises.

Itineraries: MSC Cruises offers a variety of itineraries that cover the popular ports of South America. Destinations often include Buenos Aires, Montevideo, Rio de Janeiro, and Santos. MSC also offers seasonal routes to the Galápagos Islands.

Ship Features: MSC's ships like the **MSC Preziosa** and **MSC Lirica** feature stylish, contemporary designs with luxurious staterooms and suites. The ships are equipped with modern amenities such as large pools, entertainment venues, and a variety of dining options, including Italian-themed restaurants and Mediterranean-inspired cuisine.

Experience: MSC Cruises caters to a diverse audience, including families with children, couples, and solo travelers. The cruise line offers a more affordable luxury experience compared to other premium cruise lines, with more emphasis on entertainment, dining, and onboard fun. MSC Cruises is also known for having family-friendly features like kids' clubs, water parks, and family-oriented excursions.

Regent Seven Seas Cruises

For travelers seeking an ultra-luxury experience, Regent Seven Seas Cruises offers an all-inclusive, five-star cruising experience with a focus on service, comfort, and personalized attention. The line is particularly known for its intimate ships and exclusive itineraries.

Itineraries: Regent offers select itineraries that focus on high-end explorations of South America. These cruises typically offer all-inclusive pricing, covering shore excursions, flights, and gratuities. Popular ports of call include Rio de Janeiro, Buenos Aires, and Valparaiso.

Ship Features: The ships of Regent Seven Seas, such as the **Seven Seas Mariner**, feature spacious suites, fine dining restaurants, and luxurious onboard amenities, including personalized concierge services, spa facilities, and even in-suite dining. The level of luxury onboard is unparalleled, with elegant interiors and an emphasis on comfort.

Experience: Regent is best suited for those who are looking for a truly luxurious experience. The all-inclusive pricing ensures that passengers enjoy a high level of service without worrying about additional costs. The cruise line is known for its exceptional shore excursions, which are included in the fare, offering in-depth cultural experiences in the ports visited.

Azamara Cruises

Azamara Cruises is another luxury line that focuses on more intimate, culturally enriching cruises. Azamara is known for its small-ship experience, which allows passengers to visit ports that larger ships cannot access.

Itineraries: Azamara offers a variety of itineraries in South America, including routes that stop in Buenos Aires, Rio de Janeiro, and the Falkland Islands. Azamara cruises are often longer and more leisurely, focusing on immersing passengers in the culture and nature of the destinations.

Ship Features: Azamara ships, such as the **Azamara Journey** and **Azamara Quest**, are mid-sized vessels that provide an intimate cruising experience. They offer elegant staterooms, exquisite dining, and a focus on local experiences both onboard and ashore. The ships also feature refined dining options, spa treatments, and enriching onboard activities like destination-focused lectures.

Experience: Azamara caters to a niche market of travelers who seek a blend of luxury, cultural immersion, and intimate experiences. The line's longer itineraries and focus on smaller ports make it ideal for those looking for more in-depth explorations of South America.

Types of Ships and Their Amenities

When choosing a cruise line, it's important to consider the type of ship that suits your preferences. South American cruises offer a wide range of ships, from large ocean-going vessels to smaller expedition ships designed for adventure. Here's a breakdown of the types of ships commonly found on South American itineraries:

Large Ocean Liners

Large ocean liners are the most common type of ships operating in South America. These vessels typically offer a wide variety of amenities, including multiple dining options, pools, spas, fitness centers, theaters, and shopping malls. They are perfect for travelers who enjoy luxury and comfort while cruising between popular ports. Major cruise lines like Princess Cruises, Celebrity Cruises, and MSC use these ships, which can carry anywhere from 2,000 to 5,000 passengers.

Expedition Ships

For those looking to explore more remote parts of South America, such as the Galápagos Islands or the Antarctic Peninsula, expedition ships are the ideal option. These smaller ships, like those operated by Holland America and Azamara, allow passengers to access destinations that larger ships cannot reach. They are designed with adventure in mind, often featuring Zodiac boats for shore landings, a focus on wildlife excursions, and comfortable but less opulent accommodations.

Luxury Small Ships

Luxury small ships, like those operated by Regent Seven Seas, offer a more intimate and exclusive cruising experience. These ships typically carry fewer than 1,000 passengers and provide an all-inclusive, highly personalized service. The luxury ships are equipped with spacious suites, gourmet dining, and all-inclusive shore excursions, making them ideal for those seeking a lavish and relaxed experience.

Boutique Ships

Boutique ships fall in between large ocean liners and luxury small ships, offering a more intimate experience with many of the comforts of larger vessels. These ships tend to have more specialized itineraries and may offer more unique experiences for those looking for a smaller-scale cruise without sacrificing comfort. Ships in this category include some from lines like Azamara and Oceania Cruises.

CHAPTER 5: BEST TIME TO CRUISE SOUTH AMERICA: CLIMATE AND WEATHER

When planning a cruise to South America, one of the most important considerations is timing. South America is a vast continent with diverse climates, which can vary significantly depending on the region, season, and even elevation. Understanding the weather patterns is essential to ensure that you have the best possible cruising experience. This chapter will guide you through the key climate considerations for cruising South America, helping you choose the best time to set sail, and offering insights into the specific weather conditions you can expect during your cruise.

Understanding South America's Climate Zones

South America spans a wide range of latitudes, from the tropical regions of the north to the temperate zones of the south, and from arid deserts to lush rainforests and icy tundras. As a result, the continent's climate is varied, and different regions experience different weather patterns throughout the year.

Here is an overview of the main climate zones you should be aware of when cruising South America:

Tropical Climate (Amazon Rainforest and Coastal Areas):

This climate zone is characterized by hot temperatures and high humidity year-round, with distinct wet and dry seasons. The Amazon Rainforest, for instance, has a tropical climate with frequent rainfall.

Coastal cities like Rio de Janeiro and Buenos Aires also experience a tropical climate, although the closer you are to the southern hemisphere, the milder the climate becomes.

Temperate Climate (Southern Cone, Patagonia, and Chilean Fjords):

The southern part of South America, including areas like Patagonia, Tierra del

Fuego, and the Chilean Fjords, experiences cooler temperatures and is marked by distinct seasonal changes.

The weather can be unpredictable, with strong winds, sudden rain showers, and significant temperature drops, especially during the winter months (June-August).

Mountainous Climate (Andes Mountains):

The Andes Mountains, which run along the western side of the continent, have a high-altitude climate, with cooler temperatures and even snowfall in certain regions during the colder months. Cities like Quito (Ecuador) and La Paz (Bolivia) are located in high-altitude areas and experience cooler temperatures year-round.

Desert Climate (Atacama Desert):

The Atacama Desert, located in northern Chile, is one of the driest places on Earth. This region experiences extreme temperature fluctuations, with scorching hot days and cold nights. Rain is rare, but when it occurs, it can be intense.

Now that we've established the varying climates of South America, let's dive deeper into how to plan your cruise according to the weather conditions.

Best Time to Cruise: Regional Breakdown

The best time to cruise South America depends largely on the regions you intend to visit. Different destinations have different peak seasons based on climate, weather patterns, and local holidays.

Amazon River Cruises: The Wet and Dry Seasons

The Amazon River is one of the most sought-after destinations in South America, but the experience can differ dramatically depending on the season.

Best Time to Cruise the Amazon: The best time for an Amazon River cruise is during the dry season, which typically runs from **June to November**. During this time, the river's water levels are lower, which makes it easier to explore smaller tributaries and reach deeper into the jungle. The dry season also offers fewer mosquitoes and more pleasant conditions for excursions like hiking and wildlife spotting.

Rainy Season (December to May): The rainy season in the Amazon begins in December and continues through May. While the rainfall makes the jungle more lush and vibrant, it also raises the water levels of the river, making it harder to access certain areas and limiting the excursions that can be done. However, the rainy season can also be a unique time to experience the rainforest at its most alive, with increased wildlife activity and more vibrant vegetation.

Temperature: The Amazon region remains hot and humid throughout the year. Expect daytime temperatures of **85°F to 95°F (29°C to 35°C)**, with a high level of humidity.

Coastal South America: Buenos Aires, Rio de Janeiro, and Santos

Coastal cities such as Buenos Aires, Rio de Janeiro, and Santos are popular stops on South American cruises. The best time to visit these cities depends on the weather, as well as on the holiday season, which can affect prices and crowds.

Best Time to Cruise Coastal South America: The best time for coastal cruises is typically during the Southern Hemisphere's summer months, from **December to March**. During this period, the weather is warm and comfortable, ideal for exploring the cities and enjoying the beaches. In Rio de Janeiro, you can experience the famous Carnival festival in February, which is one of the most spectacular events in the world.

Shoulder Season (March to May, September to November): If you prefer to avoid the crowds and higher prices, the shoulder season is a great option. The weather is still mild, with temperatures ranging from **70°F to 80°F (21°C to 27°C)**, though you may encounter occasional rain showers.

Winter (June to August): During the winter months, temperatures drop, especially in cities further south like Buenos Aires. The weather is cooler and less humid, but it can be rainy and less conducive to outdoor activities.

Patagonia and the Chilean Fjords: Best Time for Exploring the South

Patagonia, located at the southern tip of South America, is a must-see destination for those seeking stunning natural beauty. The Chilean Fjords are also part of the allure, with their glaciers, mountains, and fjords creating one of the most majestic landscapes on Earth.

Best Time to Cruise Patagonia and the Chilean Fjords: The best time to visit Patagonia and the Chilean Fjords is during the Southern Hemisphere's summer months, from **November to March**. This is when the region experiences milder weather, with temperatures ranging from **50°F to 60°F (10°C to 16°C)** in the south. The summer months also provide more opportunities for outdoor exploration and activities like hiking, kayaking, and wildlife viewing.

Winter (June to August): Winter is the off-season for Patagonia and the Chilean

Fjords. The weather is cold, and many of the areas become more difficult to access due to snow and rain. However, for travelers who enjoy fewer crowds and don't mind the cold, winter offers a serene and quiet environment for those who want to experience Patagonia in a more isolated way.

Wind and Weather: One thing to be prepared for when cruising through the Chilean Fjords is the wind. The region is known for strong gusts that can make the experience chilly even during the warmer months. Layered clothing is highly recommended, as temperatures can fluctuate throughout the day.

Galápagos Islands: Year-Round Weather

The Galápagos Islands, located off the coast of Ecuador, are a year-round destination for cruise travelers. The weather in the Galápagos remains fairly consistent, with temperatures typically ranging from **70°F to 85°F (21°C to 29°C)** throughout the year.

Best Time to Cruise the Galápagos Islands: The best time to visit the Galápagos is between **December and May**. During this period, the weather is warm and dry, and the seas are calmer, making it perfect for snorkeling, swimming, and kayaking. The water temperature is also warmer, which is ideal for those who enjoy exploring underwater.

Cooler Season (June to November): From June to November, the Galápagos experiences its cooler, dry season. While the weather is still pleasant, the waters can be rougher, and the visibility for snorkeling may not be as clear. However, this is the best time to see migratory birds and other wildlife, such as sea lions and penguins, in the cooler waters.

Temperature and Water Conditions: The Galápagos enjoys mild weather year-round, and while the water temperature may dip slightly during the cooler months, it's generally pleasant for those looking to snorkel with the unique marine life.

Climate and Weather Considerations by Region

Now that we've explored the best times to visit different parts of South America, let's take a closer look at how the climate affects the cruising experience, particularly in specific regions:

Tropical Regions: Warm, Humid, and Rainy

The tropical regions of South America, including the Amazon, parts of Brazil, and northern Argentina, experience year-round warmth and humidity, with a marked difference between wet and dry seasons.

While temperatures remain high throughout the year, the humidity can be oppressive in the wet season, making travel more challenging. During the dry season, it's easier to access more remote areas, and the rainforests are often at their most vibrant.

Temperate Regions: Milder, Yet Unpredictable

The temperate regions, including cities like Buenos Aires and Montevideo, experience milder weather with clear seasons. However, the weather in these areas can be unpredictable, particularly in the shoulder seasons. Though temperatures are comfortable for travel, sudden rain showers can occur, and the climate can be cool in the southern winter months, making it less ideal for beach activities.

Polar and Arctic Regions: Cold, Windy, and Remote

For those venturing into Patagonia or the Chilean Fjords, the weather can be harsh and unpredictable. Expect colder temperatures, high winds, and occasional rain. Even in summer, the weather can shift rapidly, so it's essential to pack appropriately for layering.

CHAPTER 6: SHORE EXCURSIONS AND ACTIVITIES

One of the greatest benefits of a South American cruise is the diverse array of shore excursions and activities that await you once you step off the ship. Each port of call offers something unique—whether it's exploring ancient Incan ruins, discovering stunning wildlife, or participating in adrenaline-pumping adventures. This chapter will delve into the exciting shore excursions and activities that are available across various South American destinations. You'll find everything from nature-filled excursions to cultural experiences, and there is something for every type of traveler.

Adventure Tourism: Hiking, Kayaking, and Ziplining

South America is home to some of the most incredible natural landscapes on the planet, and there are countless adventure tourism activities available for those seeking an active cruise experience. Whether you're hiking through dense rainforests, kayaking along pristine coastlines, or ziplining over lush valleys, South America's wilderness is made for outdoor enthusiasts.

Hiking in Patagonia and the Andes

Patagonia, with its awe-inspiring peaks, glaciers, and valleys, is a haven for hikers. One of the most popular trekking spots is **Torres del Paine National Park** in Chile.

Here, you can embark on several trails that offer stunning views of jagged mountains, sparkling lakes, and abundant wildlife. For a more challenging experience, the **W Trek** is one of the most famous routes, which can take 4 to 5 days to complete, depending on your pace.

In Argentina, the **Los Glaciares National Park** is home to the famous **Perito Moreno Glacier**. For the more adventurous traveler, there are trekking excursions that take you onto the glacier itself, where you can experience the ice up close and even try ice climbing.

The **Andes Mountains** stretch across multiple countries in South America, and each offers a wealth of hiking opportunities. In **Peru**, you can explore ancient Incan ruins, including the famous **Machu Picchu**. If you're cruising to the port of **Callao** (the gateway to Lima), consider taking a day trip to hike the **Inca Trail** to Machu Picchu, one of the most iconic trekking experiences in the world.

Kayaking in the Amazon River and the Galápagos Islands

Kayaking in South America's most iconic locations is an unforgettable experience. In the Amazon River, you can take guided kayak tours through the flooded forests and narrow waterways of the rainforest. Paddling through the jungle allows you to get up close to the dense vegetation and wildlife that thrive along the riverbanks. You may encounter pink dolphins, caimans, and a host of bird species.

For those cruising to the **Galápagos Islands**, kayaking is a must-do activity. The islands' crystal-clear waters and diverse marine life offer the perfect setting for exploring by kayak. Paddle through secluded coves, along rocky coastlines, and close to the iconic volcanic landscapes. It's an opportunity to get closer to the Galápagos' unique species, including sea lions, marine iguanas, and colorful fish.

Ziplining and Canopy Walks

For an adrenaline-packed experience, many cruise itineraries offer ziplining and canopy walks in the jungles of South America. The **Rainforests of Costa Rica** offer zipline excursions that let you soar through the tree canopy, providing stunning views of the lush foliage and wildlife below.

In Brazil, you can take zipline adventures in places like the **Pantanal**, the world's largest tropical wetland, where you can zip through the trees and get a bird's-eye view of the wildlife below, including capybaras, jaguars, and various species of monkeys. Canopy tours in the Amazon Rainforest are also popular, where visitors can walk high above the jungle floor and observe the wildlife from a unique vantage point.

Cultural Experiences: Wine Tours, Tango Shows, and Historical Landmarks

South America is a region steeped in history, culture, and traditions. As a result, many shore excursions focus on providing an in-depth look into the continent's rich cultural heritage. Whether you're tasting world-class wine in Argentina, learning the passionate dance of tango in Buenos Aires, or exploring ancient ruins, cultural experiences are a highlight of any South American cruise.

Wine Tours in Argentina and Chile

The wine regions of Argentina and Chile are famous worldwide for producing some of the finest wines. Both countries offer exceptional wine tours, where you can visit renowned vineyards, taste exquisite wines, and learn about the winemaking process.

Mendoza, Argentina: Mendoza, located at the foot of the Andes, is Argentina's most famous wine-producing region. Here, you can visit sprawling wineries and vineyards, enjoy wine tastings, and learn about the production of Malbec, Argentina's signature wine. Many tours also include a traditional Argentine lunch, where you can sample local dishes paired with wine.

Chile's Central Valley: Chile is home to several renowned wine regions, including the Central Valley. A wine tour in Chile can take you to famous wineries in the **Maipo Valley** or **Colchagua Valley**, where you can taste wines like Cabernet Sauvignon and Carmenere. The stunning landscape of vineyards nestled against the backdrop of the Andes adds to the appeal of the wine tours in this region.

Tango Shows and Dance Lessons in Buenos Aires

Buenos Aires is the birthplace of the tango, and no visit to the city would be complete without experiencing this passionate dance form. Several shore excursions offer tango shows, where you can enjoy live performances by professional dancers. For a truly immersive experience, consider taking a tango lesson yourself, where expert instructors guide you through the sensual steps of this famous Argentine dance.

In addition to tango, Buenos Aires offers a range of cultural experiences. Visit **La Boca**, a colorful neighborhood famous for its brightly painted houses and tango clubs. You can also explore **San Telmo**, one of the city's oldest neighborhoods, where cobblestone streets are lined with art galleries, antique shops, and traditional cafés.

Exploring Ancient Ruins in Peru and Ecuador

South America is home to some of the world's most fascinating ancient civilizations, and many shore excursions focus on exploring their impressive ruins. In Peru, the most famous archaeological site is **Machu Picchu**, the ancient Incan city located high in the Andes. Most cruises offer day trips to **Cusco** and **Machu Picchu**, where you can explore the UNESCO World Heritage site and learn about the fascinating history of the Inca Empire.

Ecuador also offers incredible historical sites, particularly the **Inca ruins of Ingapirca**. These ruins, located near the city of Cuenca, were once an important Incan outpost. Guided tours of the site offer a deep dive into the history and significance of the Incan Empire in Ecuador.

Wildlife Encounters: Penguins, Llamas, and More

South America is teeming with unique wildlife, and many shore excursions focus on providing travelers with opportunities to observe these fascinating animals in their natural habitats. Whether you're heading to the remote islands of the Galápagos or venturing into the wetlands of the Pantanal, you'll have plenty of chances to witness South America's incredible biodiversity.

Penguin Watching in the Falkland Islands and Patagonia

One of the most exciting wildlife experiences in South America is watching penguins in their natural environment. The **Falkland Islands**, located off the coast of Argentina, are home to several species of penguins, including **King Penguins**, **Magellanic Penguins**, and **Gentoo Penguins**. Penguins can often be seen waddling along the beaches or swimming in the surrounding waters. Several shore excursions take you to penguin colonies where you can observe these charming creatures up close.

In **Patagonia**, you'll find **Magellanic Penguins** nesting in the coastal areas. The **Punta Tombo Penguin Reserve** is one of the largest penguin colonies in South America and is a popular stop for cruises heading to the region. During the breeding season (October to March), visitors can walk along marked paths and get close to the penguins.

Llamas and Andean Wildlife in Peru and Bolivia

Llamas are one of the most iconic animals of the Andean region, and there are plenty of opportunities to spot them in their native habitat. In Peru, travelers can visit the high-altitude plains near **Cusco** and the **Sacred**

Valley, where they can see llamas grazing peacefully among the Inca ruins.

In **Bolivia**, the **Salar de Uyuni**, the world's largest salt flat, is home to a variety of Andean wildlife, including flamingos, vicuñas (wild relatives of the llama), and llamas themselves. Many shore excursions include guided hikes through this stunning region, where you can witness the beauty of the high-altitude desert landscape and its unique wildlife.

Wildlife in the Pantanal and the Amazon Rainforest

The **Pantanal** in Brazil is one of the best places in the world to spot wildlife. This vast wetland is home to jaguars, capybaras, caimans, and hundreds of bird species, including the vibrant **Hyacinth Macaw**. Guided wildlife safaris in the Pantanal give you the chance to see these animals in their natural habitat, either by boat or on foot.

The **Amazon Rainforest** is another incredible destination for wildlife enthusiasts. On a cruise through the Amazon River, you'll encounter an array of exotic species, from **monkeys** and **sloths** to **piranhas** and colorful **birds** like the **Scarlet Macaw**. Many Amazon River cruises include guided excursions where you can hike through the jungle, go birdwatching, or even take small boat tours to explore the remote tributaries.

Relaxation and Scenic Cruises: Wine Tastings, Spa Treatments, and Scenic Sails

Not every shore excursion needs to be action-packed. South America's beautiful scenery and laid-back atmosphere provide ample opportunities for relaxation. Whether you're indulging in a spa treatment onboard, enjoying a scenic sail through the Chilean Fjords, or unwinding with a wine tasting in Mendoza, there's no shortage of ways to relax during your cruise.

Wine Tastings and Culinary Experiences

Wine lovers can indulge in world-class tastings at some of the most famous wineries in South America, including the vineyards of **Mendoza, Argentina**, and **Chile's Central Valley**. Several shore excursions focus on culinary experiences, from cooking classes that teach you how to prepare traditional dishes like Argentine **asado** to wine-and-food pairing experiences that take place in scenic vineyard settings.

Spa Treatments and Relaxation on Board

Cruising isn't just about exploring; it's also about unwinding and enjoying some downtime. Many South American cruise ships feature luxurious spas, where you can enjoy a relaxing massage, facial, or body treatment. If you prefer to relax in a more scenic environment, many ships offer outdoor relaxation areas with sweeping views of the ocean and coastline.

Scenic Sails Through the Chilean Fjords and the Patagonian Coast

One of the most relaxing—and visually stunning—activities you can enjoy during your South American cruise is a scenic sail through the **Chilean Fjords** or along the **Patagonian coast**. As your ship glides past towering glaciers, lush forests, and jagged mountains, you'll be treated to some of the most breathtaking views of South America's natural beauty. Many cruises to this region offer a day or two of scenic sailing, providing the perfect opportunity to relax and take in the incredible surroundings.

CHAPTER 7: DINING AND CUISINE: WHAT TO EXPECT ONBOARD AND ASHORE

Food is an essential part of the South American cruise experience, both onboard the ship and when you step ashore to explore the diverse culinary traditions of this vast continent. South America offers a wealth of flavors and ingredients, influenced by indigenous cultures, colonial histories, and modern-day food trends. This chapter will guide you through the dining options available on your cruise ship and what to expect when you explore the shores of South America. Whether you're looking to indulge in regional specialties, savor gourmet international dishes, or discover the vibrant food culture of the cities and towns you visit, South America's culinary scene promises to delight every palate.

Onboard Dining: A Global Fusion of Flavors

Cruise lines that operate in South America pride themselves on offering diverse and high-quality dining experiences for their passengers. From casual buffets to fine dining restaurants, the dining options aboard a cruise ship reflect both international cuisine and regional South American influences. Many cruise lines feature multi-course meals and themed dinners, with options designed to accommodate various dietary needs and preferences.

Casual Dining and Buffets

Most cruise ships offer a casual dining experience with an international buffet that serves breakfast, lunch, and dinner. These buffets typically feature a wide range of dishes, including:

Continental breakfast options: Fresh fruit, croissants, pastries, eggs, bacon, and local specialties such as Argentine **medialunas** (sweet croissants) or Brazilian **pão de queijo** (cheese bread).

Salads and soups: A selection of fresh salads, soups, and chilled appetizers are often available for those looking for lighter options.

Carving stations and grilled meats: Many buffets have live cooking stations where chefs carve roasts of meat such as beef, pork, and chicken, often accompanied by side dishes like mashed potatoes, rice, or vegetables.

Desserts and sweets: Cruises typically offer a variety of sweet treats, including cakes, cookies, ice cream, and regional desserts like **dulce de leche** (a caramelized milk spread) or **torta de chocolate** (chocolate cake).

Cruise lines often emphasize fresh ingredients, and many ships incorporate local ingredients from the regions you're visiting into their buffet offerings. For instance, in South America, you might find fresh tropical fruits like **mango**, **papaya**, and **guava** alongside traditional international buffet items.

Specialty Dining and Fine Dining Restaurants

For passengers who prefer a more formal dining experience, most cruise ships feature specialty restaurants that offer more refined menus. These restaurants often require reservations and may incur an additional charge, but they provide an elevated culinary experience with multiple courses and impeccable service. Popular options include:

Steakhouse-style dining: Given South America's rich tradition of cattle ranching, steakhouses are a popular feature on many cruise ships. Onboard, you can expect to find high-quality cuts of meat like **filet**

mignon, **sirloin**, and **rib-eye** steaks, often served with sides such as mashed potatoes, grilled vegetables, and sauces like chimichurri (a flavorful Argentine condiment made of herbs, garlic, and vinegar).

Italian and Mediterranean options: Many cruise ships feature Italian restaurants that serve pizzas, pastas, and seafood dishes. On South American cruises, you might find seafood pastas made with fresh fish and shellfish sourced from the region's coastal waters.

Gourmet dining: High-end restaurants onboard may offer prix-fixe menus or tasting menus, which feature a variety of dishes expertly paired with wines. Expect exquisite courses such as **lobster bisque**, **pan-seared foie gras**, or **rack of lamb**, often accompanied by regional wines from Argentina, Chile, and Uruguay.

On certain luxury cruise lines, like **Regent Seven Seas** or **Oceania Cruises**, onboard dining reaches its pinnacle, with multiple specialty dining venues and renowned chefs preparing exquisite dishes inspired by global and South American cuisines. For instance, you might enjoy **ceviche** (a citrus-marinated raw fish dish) in a Peruvian-themed restaurant or indulge in a **Brazilian churrasco** (barbecue) experience with skewers of grilled meats served at your table.

Room Service and In-Suite Dining

Many cruises also offer in-suite dining or room service, allowing passengers to enjoy meals in the privacy of their cabins. Room service menus usually feature breakfast items like eggs, pastries, and fruits, as well as casual lunch and dinner options like sandwiches, salads, and pizzas. For those looking for a more private dining experience after a day of exploration, in-suite dining is a convenient and enjoyable option.

Regional South American Flavors: What to Expect Ashore

South American cuisine is incredibly diverse, reflecting the continent's unique geography and cultural heritage. Each country, and even different regions within the countries, have distinct culinary traditions. When you cruise through South America, you'll have the opportunity to try a wide range of delicious dishes influenced by the local culture, climate, and ingredients. Here's a closer look at some of the most iconic regional dishes you can expect to encounter ashore.

Argentina: Meat, Wine, and Empanadas

Argentina is a meat lover's paradise, known for its world-class steaks and barbecue. If you're stopping in Buenos Aires, **Mendoza**, or **Bariloche**, you'll experience some of the best beef in the world. Argentina's **asado** (barbecue) is a must-try, typically featuring cuts of beef like **bife de chorizo** (sirloin steak), **costillas** (ribs), and **morcilla** (blood sausage), all cooked over an open flame. These are often served with chimichurri sauce, a tangy, herb-infused condiment.

Argentina is also famous for its **empanadas**, which are savory pastries filled with ingredients like minced beef, onions, olives, and boiled eggs. **Dulce de leche**, a sweet milk-based spread, is used in many desserts, such as **alfajores** (cookie sandwiches) and **torta de dulce de leche** (caramelized milk cake).

Don't miss the opportunity to visit a **parrilla** (steakhouse) for an authentic

Argentine dining experience, where you can indulge in juicy cuts of meat and pair them with regional wines, particularly **Malbec** from Mendoza's vineyards.

Brazil: Feijoada, Seafood, and Tropical Fruits

Brazil's cuisine is a vibrant mix of African, Portuguese, and indigenous influences, with an emphasis on rice, beans, and fresh tropical ingredients. One of the most iconic dishes in Brazil is **feijoada**, a hearty stew made with black beans, pork, beef, and sausage, typically served with rice, farofa (toasted cassava flour), and **couve** (collard greens).

When cruising along Brazil's coastline, especially in **Rio de Janeiro** or **Salvador**, you'll encounter a wide variety of seafood. **Moqueca**, a flavorful Brazilian fish stew made with coconut milk, tomatoes, onions, and peppers, is a must-try. For a refreshing snack, try **açaí** bowls topped with granola and fresh fruit, or sip on **caipirinha**, Brazil's signature cocktail made with cachaça, lime, and sugar.

Tropical fruits like **mango**, **papaya**, and **guava** are commonly found in Brazilian markets and restaurants, often used in fresh juices and smoothies.

Chile: Seafood, Wine, and Pastel de Choclo

Chile, with its long coastline, is famous for its seafood, and you'll find an abundance of fresh fish, shellfish, and mollusks in dishes like **curanto** (a traditional seafood and meat stew cooked in an underground oven) and **empanadas de mariscos** (seafood-filled pastries).

Chile is also renowned for its wine, and while cruising through the country, particularly in the wine-producing **Maipo Valley**, you'll have the chance to sample world-class reds like **Cabernet Sauvignon** and **Carmenère**. Pair your wine with a plate of **pastel de choclo**, a delicious

Chilean casserole made with corn, meat, onions, and hard-boiled eggs.

Don't miss out on the opportunity to visit local markets and try Chile's famous **congrio** (conger eel), a delicacy often served fried or grilled.

Peru: Ceviche, Andean Grains, and Pisco Sour

Peruvian cuisine is one of the most diverse and exciting on the continent, influenced by a mix of indigenous, Spanish, African, and Asian flavors. **Ceviche**, a dish made from raw fish marinated in citrus juices and mixed with onions, chili peppers, and cilantro, is a must-try. In **Lima**, the country's gastronomic capital, you can enjoy **ceviche** alongside a glass of **Pisco Sour**, the country's signature cocktail made with Pisco (grape brandy), lime, egg whites, and bitters.

Peru is also known for its ancient grains, including **quinoa** and **amaranth**, which are used in both savory and sweet dishes. If you're exploring the Sacred Valley or Cusco, be sure to try **cuy** (guinea pig), a traditional Andean delicacy often served roasted or fried.

Regional Wines and Spirits

South America is home to some of the world's finest wines, particularly from Argentina and Chile. On your cruise, you'll have the opportunity to sample local wines that pair perfectly with the regional dishes you try ashore. Argentine **Malbec** and Chilean **Carmenère** are the standout varieties, but you'll also find excellent whites like **Sauvignon Blanc** and **Chardonnay**.

In addition to wine, South America offers unique spirits like **Pisco**, a grape brandy from Peru and Chile, and **Cachaça**, the main ingredient in Brazil's famous cocktail, **caipirinha**. Many cruise lines offer tastings of these spirits onboard or through shore excursions, allowing you to explore the regional drink culture in greater depth.

CHAPTER 8: SAFETY TIPS AND HEALTH PRECAUTIONS

When traveling to a continent as diverse and dynamic as South America, it's important to consider safety and health precautions in order to fully enjoy your cruise without unnecessary worries. South America offers a range of experiences, from bustling cities to remote wilderness, and while the region is home to some of the most beautiful and exciting destinations in the world, there are certain safety measures and health considerations to keep in mind.

This chapter will provide a comprehensive guide to staying safe and healthy while cruising in South America. We will cover a wide array of topics, including vaccinations, common health risks, personal safety, travel insurance, and tips for staying healthy both onboard and onshore. By following the advice outlined here, you can ensure that your South American adventure remains memorable for all the right reasons.

Health Precautions: Vaccinations and Disease Prevention

Health precautions are an essential part of preparing for any international journey, and South America is no exception. Certain regions of South America require specific vaccinations and health measures to avoid contracting diseases that may be more prevalent in tropical and rural areas. Before embarking on your cruise, it's wise to consult with a healthcare provider or travel clinic to make sure you're up to date on the necessary vaccinations and preventative treatments.

Vaccinations Recommended for South America

The following vaccinations are commonly recommended for travelers visiting South America, especially if you plan to visit rural or tropical areas:

Hepatitis A and B: Hepatitis A is a viral infection that can be contracted through contaminated food or water, while Hepatitis B is transmitted through blood and bodily fluids. Both vaccines are recommended for travel to South America.

Typhoid: Typhoid fever is a bacterial infection that is contracted by consuming contaminated food or water. This vaccination is particularly important if you're visiting remote areas, where sanitation might not be as reliable.

Yellow Fever: Yellow fever is a viral disease spread by mosquitoes. The vaccine is required for travelers to certain parts of South America, such as the Amazon Basin and some areas of Brazil and Argentina. Some countries require proof of vaccination (Yellow Fever certificate) before allowing entry. Check with your cruise line to see whether a certificate is needed.

Malaria Prevention: In areas with high malaria risk, such as the Amazon

Rainforest, you may be prescribed antimalarial medication. Consult with your doctor for the appropriate medication based on your cruise itinerary.

Tetanus, Diphtheria, and Pertussis (Tdap): A routine vaccination that you may need to update if it's been more than ten years since your last dose.

Rabies: While rabies is rare in South America, it may be recommended for travelers who are planning to visit rural or remote areas where contact with animals is likely.

Routine Vaccinations: Ensure that your routine vaccinations, such as MMR (measles, mumps, rubella), influenza, and polio, are up to date before you depart.

General Health Precautions

While vaccinations are an essential part of protecting your health, there are also additional precautions that can help prevent illness during your cruise:

Stay Hydrated: South America is known for its hot and humid climate, particularly in the Amazon Rainforest and coastal regions. It's important to drink plenty of water, especially during shore excursions. Carry a reusable water bottle and ensure you're drinking purified or bottled water, as tap water in some regions may not be safe to drink.

Avoid Raw or Undercooked Food: While South American cuisine is delicious and diverse, travelers are advised to be cautious with street food and raw or undercooked foods. Stick to hot, freshly cooked meals to reduce the risk of foodborne illnesses.

Use Insect Repellent: In areas such as the Amazon, there is a higher risk of insect-borne diseases, such as dengue fever, Zika virus, and malaria. Use an insect repellent with DEET or other effective ingredients, especially during outdoor excursions in jungle or coastal areas.

Bring Prescription Medications: If you're on prescription medications, be sure to bring enough for the duration of your trip, along with any necessary documentation for customs. It's also a good idea to carry a list of your medications and dosages in case you need to refill while abroad.

Prepare for Altitude Sickness: Some South American destinations, such as **Cusco** and **La Paz**, are located at high altitudes. If you're not accustomed to high-altitude environments, you may experience symptoms of altitude sickness, such as dizziness, headaches, and shortness of breath. Drink plenty of water, take it easy when you first arrive, and ask your doctor about medications to prevent altitude sickness.

Onboard Health and Safety: Medical Facilities, First Aid, and Security

While onboard your cruise ship, the cruise line will prioritize your health and safety by providing medical services, first-aid stations, and a variety of preventative measures. Here's what to expect:

Medical Facilities Onboard

Ship's Medical Center: Most modern cruise ships are equipped with medical facilities staffed by doctors and nurses. These clinics are designed to handle minor health issues, such as seasickness, cuts and bruises, or other non-emergency medical needs. If you have a medical emergency, the medical team will work with local hospitals in port to provide care.

Seasickness: If you're prone to seasickness, be sure to bring motion sickness medications or patches (such as **Dramamine** or **Scopolamine**). You can also ask the ship's medical team for remedies to help alleviate the symptoms.

Onboard Safety Measures: Cruise ships are equipped with a variety of safety measures to protect passengers in the event of an emergency. These include life jackets, lifeboats, and detailed evacuation procedures, which will be demonstrated to you during the mandatory safety drill upon embarkation.

Cruise Line Health Protocols: In light of the COVID-19 pandemic, many cruise lines have implemented enhanced health and safety protocols, including increased sanitation, contactless services, and health screenings. Make sure to stay informed of any updates related to your cruise and follow the guidelines set by the cruise line.

Personal Safety and Security Onboard

Your cruise line will take measures to ensure the safety of its passengers, including security staff, surveillance systems, and access control to different areas of the ship. However, as with any public space, it's important to stay vigilant:

Keep Personal Belongings Secure: Use the safe in your cabin to store valuables like passports, credit cards, and electronics. Avoid leaving items unattended in public areas.

Be Aware of Scams: Though rare, it's possible to encounter scams, particularly in popular ports. Always use trusted taxi services, avoid carrying large sums of cash, and only book excursions through the cruise line to ensure you're dealing with reputable operators.

Follow Safety Briefings: Pay attention to the safety briefings at the beginning of your cruise, and familiarize yourself with the locations of emergency exits, lifeboats, and muster stations.

Safety onshore: Personal Safety Tips and Crime Prevention

While South America is an exciting and diverse region to explore, it's important to be aware of potential safety concerns when venturing ashore. Like any popular tourist destination, some areas of South America may have higher crime rates, particularly in certain cities. However, with proper precautions, you can minimize risk and enjoy a safe and rewarding experience.

General Safety Tips for Shore Excursions

Stay in Groups: Whenever possible, stay in groups, particularly during excursions or when visiting unfamiliar areas. If you're exploring a city, it's a good idea to take organized tours with a reputable guide rather than venturing off on your own.

Use Reputable Transportation: Always use trusted transportation options. In major cities like Buenos Aires, Rio de Janeiro, or Lima, taxis are generally safe, but ensure they are from authorized taxi stands or use ride-hailing apps like **Uber**.

Keep Valuables Secure: Pickpocketing can occur in crowded areas, so keep your valuables secure and out of sight. Use a money belt or a neck pouch for important items like your passport, cash, and credit cards.

Be Cautious in Crowded Areas: Tourist hotspots, markets, and busy streets can attract pickpockets and petty criminals. Always be mindful of your surroundings and avoid displaying valuable items like expensive jewelry or electronics.

Avoid Remote or High-Crime Areas: While South America is home to many safe and welcoming destinations, certain neighborhoods, particularly in large cities, may have higher crime rates. Always check with your cruise line or local authorities about areas to avoid, and plan your excursions accordingly.

Emergency Numbers and Contact Information

Emergency Services: In case of emergencies, know the local emergency numbers for police, fire, and medical services in the country you are visiting. For most of South America, the general emergency number is **911**, but it's good to check with your cruise line or local guides upon arrival.

Embassy Contacts: Keep a list of your country's embassy or consulate numbers, as well as emergency contact information for your cruise line.

Travel Insurance: Protecting Yourself and Your Trip

Travel insurance is a vital consideration when cruising in South America. While the region is generally safe, travel insurance can protect you in the event of unforeseen circumstances, such as a medical emergency, trip cancellation, lost luggage, or missed connections.

What Travel Insurance Should Cover

Medical Coverage: Make sure your insurance policy includes medical coverage for emergencies while abroad, including the costs of evacuation if necessary. Medical treatment in certain remote regions of South America may be expensive or hard to access, so having proper coverage is essential.

Trip Cancellation: If you need to cancel or interrupt your trip due to illness, family emergencies, or other covered reasons, trip cancellation insurance can help you recover some of your expenses.

Lost Luggage and Travel Delays: Coverage for lost luggage, trip delays, or missed connections can save you money and stress if your belongings are delayed or lost.

Emergency Evacuation: If you're traveling to more remote areas (like the Amazon or Patagonia), consider a policy that covers emergency evacuation, as medical services in these regions can be limited.

CHAPTER 9: MONEY MATTERS: BUDGETING FOR A SOUTH AMERICA CRUISE

Embarking on a South American cruise offers an incredible array of experiences, from exploring vibrant cities and ancient ruins to discovering natural wonders like the Amazon Rainforest and Patagonia. However, like any international travel, it's essential to manage your finances and plan your budget accordingly. Understanding the cost structure of your cruise and how to handle expenses while ashore will ensure that your journey is smooth and stress-free.

This chapter will guide you through the financial aspects of cruising in South America. We'll cover how to budget for your trip, what to expect in terms of costs, and practical tips for handling money, including currency exchange, tipping, and managing onboard expenses. Whether you're looking to save money or splurge on luxury experiences, this chapter will provide you with all the necessary tools to make informed financial decisions on your South American adventure.

Cruise Costs: What's Included and What's Extra

Before setting sail, it's important to have a clear understanding of what is included in the cost of your South American cruise and what additional costs you should be prepared for. Cruise packages vary greatly depending on the cruise line, ship, and itinerary, so it's crucial to read the fine print and understand the breakdown of your cruise expenses.

What's Typically Included in Your Cruise Fare

Accommodation: The price of your cruise typically includes your stateroom, ranging from basic inside cabins to luxurious suites. Your cruise fare will cover the cost of your room for the duration of the trip, including any amenities in your stateroom such as toiletries, linens, and daily housekeeping.

Meals and Dining: Most cruise lines offer a variety of dining options, with meals included in your fare. This often includes buffet-style dining, room service (though some cruise lines may charge extra for this), and meals in the main dining rooms. Onboard dining options typically feature a wide range of international cuisines, as well as regional dishes inspired by the countries you'll visit.

Specialty Restaurants: While many dining options are included, upscale dining experiences like specialty restaurants often incur an additional charge. For example, gourmet steakhouses, sushi bars, or wine-pairing dinners may require an extra fee, which can range from $20 to $75 per person, depending on the cruise line and the level of exclusivity.

Entertainment and Activities: Entertainment, such as Broadway-style shows, live music, comedy performances, and dance parties, is often included in your cruise fare. Some ships also offer various recreational activities such as poolside movies, fitness classes, trivia competitions, and onboard lectures—all of which are typically part of the package.

Port Fees and Taxes: The cost of port fees and taxes is generally included in your initial cruise fare. These fees help cover the cost of docking and other logistical expenses incurred when a ship docks at various ports along the way. These fees are often pre-paid as part of the cruise package, but you should confirm this with your cruise line before sailing.

What's Not Included in Your Cruise Fare

Alcoholic Beverages: While some cruise lines include alcoholic drinks as part of their all-inclusive packages, most will charge extra for alcoholic beverages such as wine, beer, spirits, and cocktails. Drink packages are available for purchase, which can help you save on alcohol costs, but these packages vary by cruise line.

Excursions and Shore Activities: Shore excursions are typically not included in your cruise fare. These excursions— ranging from city tours and cultural experiences to adventurous activities like zip-lining or hiking—are additional costs. Prices can vary widely depending on the activity, with shore excursions generally costing between $50 and $300 per person, depending on the duration and exclusivity of the experience.

Gratuities and Tips: While tips for dining staff and housekeeping may be included in your fare, many cruise lines add a daily gratuity fee to your onboard account, typically between $12 and $20 per person per day. This charge covers tips for the crew, including waitstaff, housekeeping, and other service employees. Some cruise lines allow passengers to adjust the gratuity charge, while others may have it as a fixed amount.

Spa and Wellness Services: Spa treatments, fitness classes, and wellness services are often available for an extra charge. Massages, facials, and other treatments can range from $50 to $150 or more, depending on the service and the ship's luxury level. Specialized classes like yoga or Pilates may also have additional fees.

Onboard Shopping and Souvenirs: Many cruise ships feature onboard shops that sell luxury goods, clothing, jewelry, cosmetics, and souvenirs. Keep in mind that these items can be priced higher than you might find in local stores, so if you plan to shop onboard, it's essential to factor this into your budget.

Shore Excursions: Planning and Budgeting for Onshore Activities

One of the highlights of a South American cruise is the opportunity to explore various destinations ashore. Whether you're wandering through Buenos Aires, hiking in Patagonia, or visiting the Galápagos Islands, shore excursions are often a key part of the experience.

Types of Shore Excursions

Cultural Tours: These excursions typically include city sightseeing tours, visits to historical landmarks, and cultural performances. For example, you may explore the tango culture in Buenos Aires or visit historical Incan ruins in Peru. Prices for these types of tours typically range from $50 to $150 per person.

Wildlife and Nature Tours: South America is home to some of the world's most diverse ecosystems, and many shore excursions focus on exploring these environments. You can take wildlife safaris in the Pantanal or Galápagos, go hiking in Patagonia, or explore the Amazon Rainforest. Prices for wildlife tours can vary depending on the length and location of the excursion, typically ranging from $100 to $250.

Adventure Tours: For those seeking an adrenaline rush, there are many adventure-based excursions such as zip-lining in the Andes, kayaking in the fjords, or snorkeling with sea lions in the Galápagos. These excursions tend to be on the more expensive side, typically ranging from $150 to $350 per person, depending on the activity and duration.

Beach and Relaxation: Some travelers may prefer more laid-back shore excursions, like visiting pristine beaches in Brazil or relaxing at luxury resorts in Chile. These excursions can often be a bit more affordable, with prices generally ranging from $50 to $100 per person for beach transfers and access to private beach clubs.

How to Budget for Shore Excursions

While it's tempting to book every shore excursion available, it's important to plan and prioritize based on your interests and budget. Here are a few tips for managing your excursion costs:

Research Excursions in Advance: Cruise lines typically list available excursions on their websites before departure. You can often book excursions in advance at a discount, so be sure to browse the options and decide which activities you're most interested in.

Book Early to Save: Booking excursions early, either through the cruise line or independent operators, can sometimes save you money. Cruise lines often offer discounts for early bookings or bundle deals for multiple excursions.

Consider Independent Tours: While cruise-sponsored excursions are convenient, booking with local guides or independent tour operators can often be cheaper. Just make sure the tours are reputable and align with the ship's schedule to ensure you're back in time for departure.

Create an Excursion Budget: Decide how many excursions you would like to take and allocate a portion of your overall cruise budget for these activities. Keep in mind that most excursions do not include meals, so it's a good idea to factor in any additional costs.

Currency Considerations: How to Handle Money While Cruising

When cruising South America, it's important to understand the currency systems of the countries you'll be visiting and how to handle your money while onshore. Some South American countries use their own local currencies, while others accept U.S. dollars. Understanding how to manage your money in port cities and remote areas will help you avoid unnecessary stress.

Currency in South America

Argentina: The official currency is the **Argentine peso (ARS)**, though U.S. dollars are commonly accepted in tourist areas.

However, be aware that exchange rates may not be favorable when paying in dollars, so it's better to use pesos if possible.

Brazil: The official currency is the **Brazilian real (BRL)**, and it is best to use reais for most transactions. Although U.S. dollars are sometimes accepted, it's not universal, and you may receive a poor exchange rate.

Chile: The official currency is the **Chilean peso (CLP)**, and it's advisable to use pesos when making purchases. While U.S. dollars are accepted in some tourist areas, the exchange rate may not be ideal.

Peru: The official currency is the **Peruvian nuevo sol (PEN)**, but U.S. dollars are widely accepted in major cities like Lima and Cusco. However, always check the exchange rate before paying in dollars.

Ecuador: Ecuador uses the **U.S. dollar (USD)** as its official currency, so you won't need to exchange money when cruising through this country.

Handling Money Onshore

Currency Exchange: It's a good idea to exchange some money before leaving your home country, especially if you'll be visiting places where credit cards are not widely accepted. Many cruise lines also offer currency exchange services onboard, though the exchange rates may not be favorable. You can also exchange money at banks or currency exchange offices in port cities.

Credit and Debit Cards: Credit cards are widely accepted in South America's major cities and tourist areas. Ensure that your card has no foreign transaction fees, and inform your bank of your travel plans to avoid your card being flagged for fraud. However, for small purchases or in more remote areas, it's always good to have cash on hand.

ATMs: ATMs are widely available in major cities and tourist hubs. However, be aware of foreign transaction fees and check with your bank regarding any fees for international withdrawals. Always use

ATMs located in well-lit, secure areas, preferably inside bank branches or malls.

Tipping: Tipping is customary in many South American countries, and while tipping practices may vary, it's important to budget for gratuities. In restaurants, a 10-15% tip is common, though it may already be included in your bill. For hotel staff and tour guides, a small tip is appreciated.

Travel Insurance: Protecting Your Finances

Travel insurance is an essential investment when cruising in South America, as it provides financial protection in case of unforeseen events such as medical emergencies, trip cancellations, or lost baggage. Travel insurance can help cover some of the costs associated with unexpected situations, allowing you to focus on enjoying your vacation rather than worrying about financial setbacks.

Types of Coverage to Consider

Trip Cancellation and Interruption Insurance: This covers you in case you need to cancel or interrupt your cruise due to unforeseen events such as illness, a family emergency, or a natural disaster.

Medical and Emergency Evacuation Insurance: Medical emergencies can be expensive, especially in remote areas. Travel insurance that includes medical coverage and emergency evacuation will help protect you if you need medical care or are required to be evacuated to a hospital.

Baggage Loss and Delay Coverage: If your luggage is delayed or lost, travel insurance can help cover the cost of replacing essential items and provide compensation for your inconvenience.

CHAPTER 10: PACKING FOR A
SOUTH AMERICA CRUISE

Packing for a South America cruise requires careful planning, as the continent offers a wide variety of climates, landscapes, and activities that can all impact what you need to bring. Whether you're cruising through the tropical Amazon Rainforest, hiking in Patagonia's chilly winds, or enjoying the warm coastal beaches of Brazil, it's essential to pack wisely to ensure that you are comfortable, well-prepared, and stylish for your adventure.

This chapter will provide you with a comprehensive packing guide, offering specific suggestions for each region you'll visit and activities you'll likely encounter. From clothing and accessories to health-related items and travel gear, we'll cover everything you need to pack to make your South American cruise unforgettable.

Essential Packing Guidelines: What to Bring

When preparing for a South American cruise, the goal is to be versatile, practical, and comfortable. You'll need to pack clothes and accessories that allow you to transition between different activities, from formal dinners on the cruise ship to adventurous excursions ashore. Here's a breakdown of essential items you should include in your packing list.

Clothing for Varying Climates

Since South America spans multiple climate zones, it's crucial to pack for both warm and cool weather, especially if your itinerary takes you through diverse regions.

Tropical and Coastal Regions (e.g., Amazon, Rio de Janeiro, Buenos Aires): For destinations with tropical or temperate climates, such as the Amazon and coastal cities like Rio de Janeiro, pack lightweight, breathable clothing that will keep you cool and comfortable. This includes:

Light, moisture-wicking shirts: Choose materials like cotton or performance fabrics to keep sweat at bay.

Lightweight pants and shorts: Loose-fitting and breathable fabrics are ideal for hot and humid weather.

Sunscreen-friendly clothing: Long-sleeve shirts and pants made of lightweight fabric can protect you from sunburn while still keeping you cool.

Swimwear: Don't forget swimsuits for beach stops or onboard pools.

Sunhat and sunglasses: To protect your face and eyes from the intense sun.

Cooler and High-Altitude Regions (e.g., Patagonia, Andes, Chilean Fjords): For destinations like Patagonia or the Andes, where temperatures can be chilly even in the summer, you'll need warmer clothing. Some areas also experience unpredictable weather, so it's important to be prepared for all conditions:

Waterproof jacket: Essential for rainy days or windy conditions.

Fleece or insulated jacket: Perfect for chilly mornings and evenings in Patagonia.

Thermal underwear: If you're planning to hike or explore high-altitude areas, packing thermals will keep you warm.

Sturdy hiking boots: If you plan to explore rugged terrain, opt for waterproof boots with good ankle support.

Layering system: When packing for cold climates, layering is key. Choose items like long-sleeve base layers, insulating mid-layers, and waterproof outer layers to stay warm and comfortable.

Evening Wear for Formal Nights: While casual attire is typical during most days on a cruise, many cruise lines offer formal nights for special dinners and events. Consider bringing at least one outfit for these occasions:

Men: A suit or a dress shirt with slacks; a tie may be optional depending on the cruise line.

Women: A cocktail dress, evening gown, or a chic dressy outfit.

Footwear for Different Activities

Footwear is one of the most important considerations for your packing list. Depending on your planned activities, you'll need a variety of shoes:

Comfortable walking shoes: For exploring ports, city tours, and shore excursions, comfortable and supportive walking shoes are essential. Sneakers or casual walking shoes that provide good arch support are ideal for most activities.

Sturdy hiking boots: If your cruise itinerary includes excursions to mountainous regions or rugged terrain (like Patagonia or the Andes), make sure you bring sturdy, waterproof boots.

Flip-flops or sandals: For beach days, poolside lounging, or relaxing in tropical regions, flip-flops or sandals are lightweight and easy to pack.

Dress shoes: For formal dinners or events, pack a pair of dress shoes or stylish sandals to complement your evening wear.

Accessories and Gear

Waterproof bags and cases: If you're exploring tropical regions like the Amazon or taking part in water-based excursions like kayaking or boat rides, waterproof bags are a smart addition. A dry bag or waterproof phone case can keep your valuables safe and dry during excursions.

Binoculars: For wildlife and scenic viewing, especially when cruising through areas like the Galápagos Islands, Chilean Fjords, or the Amazon, binoculars will enhance your experience. Bring a lightweight, compact pair for easy travel.

Camera and spare memory cards: South America offers some of the most photogenic landscapes and cultural experiences in the world. Pack a good-quality camera to capture everything, and bring extra memory cards to store all of your photos.

Power bank: While many ships have charging stations, it's always a good idea to bring a portable charger or power bank to keep your devices powered up when you're out on shore excursions.

Travel adapter: South American countries may have different electrical plug types, so make sure to bring a travel adapter to charge your electronics.

Health and Wellness: Staying Safe and Comfortable

Maintaining your health and wellness during your South American cruise is crucial to having an enjoyable experience. Packing health essentials will ensure that you are prepared for common travel-related challenges like dehydration, illness, or motion sickness.

Health Essentials

Sunscreen: The sun can be intense, especially in the tropical regions of South America. Be sure to pack a high SPF sunscreen to protect your skin during outdoor activities.

Insect repellent: In areas like the Amazon, where mosquitoes are common, packing insect repellent with DEET is essential to prevent bites and reduce the risk of insect-borne diseases.

Motion sickness medication: If you're prone to seasickness, bring motion sickness tablets or patches (such as **Dramamine** or **Scopolamine**). Cruise ships are typically stable, but for more challenging conditions (like rough seas in the southern parts of South America), having medication on hand will keep you comfortable.

Prescription medications: If you take prescription medications, make sure to bring an adequate supply for the duration of your trip. It's also a good idea to carry a doctor's note for any medications you need to bring, especially if they are not commonly found in South America.

First aid kit: A small first aid kit with essentials such as band-aids, antiseptic wipes, pain relievers (like aspirin or ibuprofen), and cold/flu medication can be helpful in case you need minor treatment onboard or ashore.

Hand sanitizer and wipes: Keeping hand sanitizer and disinfectant wipes on hand is especially important for maintaining hygiene during travel, especially if you're visiting areas with less access to soap and water.

Vaccination and Travel Health Records

It's essential to prepare your health for travel. In addition to bringing necessary medications, check with your doctor for any required vaccinations. For instance, some areas of South America may require **Yellow Fever vaccination**, especially if you're heading into remote regions like the Amazon. It's helpful to carry a health record and vaccination card with you.

Important Travel Documents and Paperwork

Before you leave for your South American cruise, ensure that you have all your important documents and paperwork ready. This includes everything needed for boarding the cruise ship and entering various countries. Packing these documents securely is vital to ensure a smooth embarkation and journey.

Passport: Your passport must be valid for at least six months beyond the date of your expected return from your cruise. Check the passport requirements for each country you'll visit and ensure you bring your passport with you for all shore excursions.

Visas: Depending on the countries you'll be visiting, you may need to obtain a visa before departure. Research visa requirements and make sure you have the proper documentation.

Cruise Tickets and Itinerary: Have a printed copy of your cruise tickets, itinerary, and any boarding passes or pre-cruise documentation. Keep these accessible for check-in at the port.

Travel Insurance: While optional, travel insurance is highly recommended. Keep a copy of your travel insurance policy and contact details for emergencies.

Vaccination Cards: Some countries in South America may require proof of vaccinations, especially if you're traveling to areas with specific health risks. Bring your vaccination record and any relevant health certificates with you.

Credit Cards and Local Currency: Bring at least one credit card and some local currency for purchases ashore. It's advisable to carry a mix of payment options, including a small amount of cash for tips and souvenirs.

Packing Tips for a Smooth Cruise Experience

Packing for a South American cruise may seem daunting, but by following a few simple tips, you can make the process easier and ensure you have everything you need for a smooth trip:

Roll Your Clothes: To maximize space in your suitcase, roll your clothes rather than folding them. This helps reduce wrinkles and frees up space for additional items.

Pack for Flexibility: Plan to bring clothing that can be layered. This will allow you to adjust based on the weather and activities you'll be doing. Layers are essential for both warm tropical climates and cooler mountain regions.

Label Your Luggage: Clearly label your luggage with your name, cruise ship, and cabin number. This makes it easier to identify and track your bags in case they get lost.

Check Cruise Line Restrictions: Review the cruise line's baggage policy for weight limits and size restrictions. Some lines may have specific rules about carry-ons or restricted items.

Pack Extra Bags for Souvenirs: South America is known for its vibrant markets and artisan crafts. Consider packing an extra foldable bag or a tote for souvenirs, so you don't run out of space for your purchases.

CHAPTER 11: CONCLUSION: MAKING THE MOST OF YOUR SOUTH AMERICA CRUISE

Embarking on a South America cruise is a journey of discovery, adventure, and cultural immersion. This diverse continent offers everything from pristine beaches and lush jungles to snow-capped mountains and vibrant cities. Whether you're looking to explore historical landmarks, sample world-class cuisine, or witness some of the most unique wildlife on Earth, South America delivers an unparalleled cruising experience. However, to truly make the most of your South American cruise, it's important to approach the trip with the right mindset, preparation, and attitude.

In this concluding chapter, we will summarize the essential tips and insights to help you make the most of your cruise. We'll revisit the key points discussed throughout the guide and provide actionable advice for ensuring that your cruise is filled with unforgettable experiences, personal growth, and smooth sailing.

Prepare for Diversity: South America's Uniqueness Awaits

South America is a continent of contrasts, and one of the best aspects of cruising in this region is the ability to experience such a wide variety of landscapes, cultures, and environments. From the tropical rainforests of the Amazon to the glaciers of Patagonia, each stop on your cruise offers a unique opportunity to explore a new world.

Before you embark, take time to familiarize yourself with the destinations you'll be visiting. Research the cultures, traditions, and history of the countries, cities, and regions on your itinerary. Understanding the cultural nuances and local customs will not only enhance your experience but also show respect for the people and places you visit.

You'll experience bustling cities like Buenos Aires and Rio de Janeiro, famous for their art, music, and food scenes. You'll also encounter nature like never before—whether it's gazing at the towering peaks of Patagonia, cruising through the Chilean Fjords, or trekking through the dense jungles of the Amazon.

Remember that each destination has its own rhythm, pace, and way of life. Approach your cruise with an open mind and be ready to adapt to different climates, time zones, and cultural norms. It's this diversity that makes South America a captivating place to explore, and you'll want to savor every moment of it.

Be Adventurous: Embrace the Journey

One of the best ways to make the most of your South American cruise is to embrace the sense of adventure that comes with traveling through such a vibrant, dynamic continent. Whether it's zip-lining through the Amazon Rainforest, trekking to Machu Picchu, or kayaking through the fjords of

Chile, there's no shortage of thrilling experiences waiting for you.

South America offers a wealth of outdoor activities for adventure enthusiasts. Some of the most exciting moments of your cruise may come from unexpected excursions or activities. For example, in the Galápagos Islands, you could find yourself swimming with sea lions or snorkeling with vibrant fish. In Patagonia, you might embark on a glacier trek, experiencing the stunning beauty of the region's frozen landscapes.

Being open to new experiences is key to getting the most out of your trip. While you might not enjoy every activity (and that's okay!), taking part in a variety of excursions will enrich your understanding of South America and give you the chance to connect with its natural wonders.

Whether you choose to venture into the heart of the Amazon, hike along the trails of Patagonia, or explore colonial towns and modern cities, every adventure will help you uncover a new side of South America.

Prioritize Cultural Immersion: Learn from the Locals

A South American cruise is not just about sightseeing—it's also about connecting with the cultures, traditions, and people of the region. South America is rich in history, culture, and diversity, and the best way to immerse yourself is by engaging with the locals and learning about their way of life.

When you're ashore, take time to explore the local markets, attend traditional performances, and taste the regional cuisines. In Buenos Aires, you could learn the passionate steps of tango or explore the city's historic neighborhoods. In Rio de Janeiro, you can attend a samba show or visit the colorful favelas to witness life in one of the city's most vibrant communities.

South America's indigenous communities, such as those in the Andes or the Amazon Basin, offer incredible opportunities to learn about ancient cultures and their traditional ways of life. Many cruises offer excursions to remote villages or cultural centers where you can engage with indigenous people, learn about their customs, and gain insight into their worldview.

Moreover, the people of South America are incredibly friendly and welcoming. A simple conversation, whether through a translator or by learning a few phrases in Spanish or Portuguese, can go a long way in creating memorable interactions. Embrace these moments—they will add depth to your experience and help you truly understand the heart of South America.

Taste the Flavors of South America: A Culinary Adventure

Food is a central part of South American culture, and your cruise is an opportunity to indulge in some of the best cuisine the continent has to offer. Whether you're dining onboard the ship or exploring local eateries ashore, South America's diverse culinary traditions are sure to excite your taste buds.

Onboard your cruise, you'll find a fusion of international flavors and regional specialties. Cruise ships cater to a wide variety of tastes, offering everything from buffets with a mix of global dishes to specialty restaurants that focus on regional South American cuisines. Be sure to try the

Argentine steaks, Brazilian feijoada (black bean stew), Chilean seafood, and Peruvian ceviche. Many cruises even offer wine-tasting excursions, where you can sample world-class wines from Argentina and Chile's famous vineyards.

While onshore, don't miss the chance to explore local markets, food festivals, and street food. In cities like Buenos Aires and Lima, food is not just sustenance—it's an experience. South America's regional cuisines vary dramatically, so there's always something new and exciting to try. Consider joining cooking classes to learn how to prepare traditional dishes or sample local delicacies with the guidance of expert chefs.

For those who appreciate fine wines, South America's wine regions offer some of the world's best vineyards. In Argentina's Mendoza region or Chile's Maipo Valley, wine-tasting tours offer a chance to learn about the region's winemaking techniques and enjoy some of the finest wines paired with local cheeses and meats.

Stay Healthy: Health Precautions and Well-Being

Ensuring your health and safety is paramount for an enjoyable cruise experience. South America presents unique health considerations depending on the regions you're visiting, so it's essential to take necessary precautions before and during your trip.

First and foremost, make sure you're up-to-date on all recommended vaccinations and health checks before traveling. Vaccines for diseases like **Hepatitis A**, **Typhoid**, **Yellow Fever**, and **Malaria** may be necessary, especially if you're traveling to tropical regions such as the Amazon or the Pantanal. Always consult your doctor or travel clinic to get personalized health advice for the areas you'll be visiting.

While onboard, take advantage of the ship's medical facilities and onboard wellness programs. Many cruises offer health and fitness services, including gym facilities, yoga classes, and even spa treatments to help you unwind. Don't forget to pack any necessary prescription medications, and carry them in their original containers, clearly labeled.

On shore, be mindful of food and water safety. In some parts of South America, drinking tap water or consuming raw food may pose a health risk, so always opt for bottled water and avoid street food that isn't prepared in front of you.

Stay Safe: Personal Safety and Security Tips

Personal safety is crucial while traveling in South America, as with any international destination. Fortunately, most regions in South America are safe for tourists, but there are some precautions you should take to ensure a secure experience.

When cruising in South America, follow basic safety protocols both onboard and ashore:

Onboard Safety: Always attend the mandatory safety briefing at the beginning of your cruise. Know the locations of lifeboats, emergency exits, and muster stations. Secure your valuables in your cabin's safe and keep an eye on your personal belongings while in public areas.

Ashore Safety: Stay in groups when exploring cities, especially after dark. Avoid displaying expensive jewelry or electronics in public, as this can attract unwanted attention. When taking taxis or ridesharing services, use reputable companies recommended by your cruise line.

Emergency Preparedness: Familiarize yourself with local emergency numbers and procedures. The general emergency number for most of South America is **911**, but check with the cruise line for specific information about the ports you will visit.

Maximize Your Experience: Plan Ahead and Be Flexible

One of the best ways to ensure you're making the most of your South American cruise is to plan ahead. Research the ports and activities you'll be visiting, and book excursions or dining experiences in advance if possible. This will save you time and allow you to secure spots in popular activities.

However, also remain flexible. South America is a region of rich diversity, and sometimes unplanned experiences turn out to be the most rewarding. Take time to explore local cafes, art galleries, and shops at your own pace. Interact with locals, ask questions, and take a break from the structured itinerary to discover something new.

A key part of cruising is balancing planning and spontaneity. The combination of structured activities and free time allows you to enjoy both planned excursions and moments of personal discovery.

Printed in Dunstable, United Kingdom